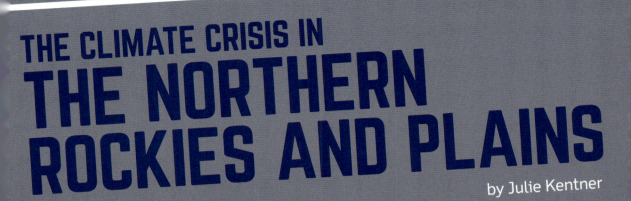

# THE CLIMATE CRISIS IN THE NORTHERN ROCKIES AND PLAINS

by Julie Kentner

**FOCUS READERS.**
NAVIGATOR

# WWW.FOCUSREADERS.COM

Copyright © 2024 by Focus Readers®, Lake Elmo, MN 55042. All rights reserved. No part of this book may be reproduced or utilized in any form or by any means without written permission from the publisher.

Focus Readers is distributed by North Star Editions:
sales@northstareditions.com | 888-417-0195

Produced for Focus Readers by Red Line Editorial.

Content Consultant: Doug Kluck, Central Region Climate Services Director for the National Oceanic and Atmospheric Administration

Photographs ©: Jacob W. Frank/National Park Services, cover, 1, 7; Matthew Brown/AP Images, 4–5; Jeff Zylland/National Park Services, 8–9; Red Line Editorial, 11; Shutterstock Images, 13, 14–15, 16, 22–23, 25, 27; Mark Thonhoff/Bureau of Land Management, 18; Kristian Buus/Alamy, 21; Tom Stromme/The Bismarck Tribune/AP Images, 28

**Library of Congress Cataloging-in-Publication Data**
Library of Congress Cataloging-in-Publication Data is available on the Library of Congress website.

**ISBN**
978-1-63739-631-5 (hardcover)
978-1-63739-688-9 (paperback)
978-1-63739-796-1 (ebook pdf)
978-1-63739-745-9 (hosted ebook)

Printed in the United States of America
Mankato, MN
082023

# ABOUT THE AUTHOR

Julie Kentner is a writer who loves history, geography, archaeology, travel, and research. She lives with her husband and their cats.

# TABLE OF CONTENTS

**CHAPTER 1**

## Montana Floods  5

**CHAPTER 2**

## Mountains and Plains  9

**CHAPTER 3**

## The Region in Crisis  15

**THAT'S AMAZING!**

## Dallas Goldtooth  20

**CHAPTER 4**

## Slowing and Adapting  23

Focus on the Northern Rockies and Plains • 30
Glossary • 31
To Learn More • 32
Index • 32

# CHAPTER 1

# MONTANA FLOODS

Montana's spring was cool in 2022. This meant the snow in the mountains melted more slowly than usual. In mid-June, temperatures got warmer. The snow started to melt. Then heavy rains fell quickly.

The rain and melted snow caused record-breaking floods. The water

**Floodwater in June 2022 destroyed and flooded many homes in Red Lodge, Montana.**

damaged hundreds of homes and businesses in several counties. The town of Red Lodge was hit hard. Roads and bridges were washed away.

People were not prepared for the emergency. Thousands of people lost power. They also lost access to clean drinking water. More than 10,000 people had to leave Yellowstone National Park. The floods set records in the region. Full recovery was expected to take years.

Scientists have linked **climate change** to shifts in the region's weather patterns. Some changes include less snow in winter at lower elevations. Changes can also mean more snow and rain in spring.

The 2022 floods damaged several roads running through Yellowstone National Park.

Flooding can happen when rain falls on the snow. The rain can cause the snow to melt quickly. This means more flooding could happen in the region in the future.

## CHAPTER 2

# MOUNTAINS AND PLAINS

**W**eather is what happens from day to day. It includes air temperature, **humidity**, **precipitation**, wind, and more. Climate also measures these things. But it measures weather patterns over many years.

Climates vary in the northern Rockies and plains. For example, North Dakota,

**North Dakota is home to Theodore Roosevelt National Park. Grasslands are the park's most common habitat.**

South Dakota, and Nebraska are part of the Great Plains. These states have grasslands. They often experience hot summers and cold winters.

The climate of the Rocky Mountains is different. These mountains span Montana and Wyoming. They reach heights of more than 12,000 feet (3,660 m). The mountains tend to have cool summers and cold winters. The winters are often snowy.

Snow in the mountains is called snowpack. The snowpack builds from October to April. Then it melts in the spring and summer. This water fills the rivers and **reservoirs** in the region and beyond. The water provides a valuable resource for millions of people.

The amount of precipitation differs across the region. Wyoming usually

## THE NORTHERN ROCKIES AND PLAINS

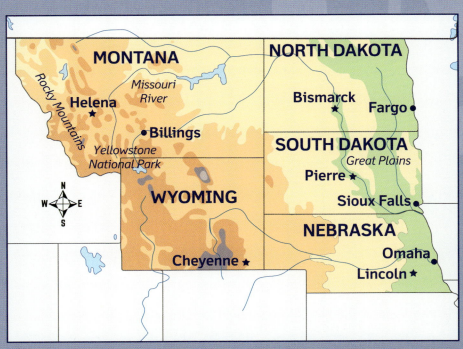

receives less rain than the other states. Nebraska gets the most precipitation in spring and early summer. Parts of Montana get the most snow in winter and spring.

## CLIMATE, BISON, AND FIRE

For thousands of years, **Indigenous** peoples have hunted bison. Some groups used climate patterns to hunt. In what is now Montana, people would set fires in the spring and fall. Those seasons often have more rain. Grass grows better if there is a lot of rain after a fire. Bison often came to eat the new grass. This would bring the bison nearby. Then people could hunt them. The bison's meat could feed many people.

A thunderstorm rages across the Badlands of South Dakota.

The northern Rockies and plains also experience many weather events. In the winter, the region can face blizzards. Then snow sometimes melts quickly. That can cause floods, mainly in the spring. In the summer, thunderstorms happen throughout the region. Sometimes these storms produce tornadoes or hail.

CHAPTER 3

# THE REGION IN CRISIS

The northern Rockies and plains are already experiencing climate change. Since 1900, average temperatures have been rising. Average low temperatures are rising faster than average highs. Also, winter temperatures are rising faster than summer temperatures. But summers are still having more hot days.

**Rising winter temperatures are melting snowpack in the northern Rockies.**

 By 2050, North Dakota could average 50 days a year with dangerous heat.

Hotter weather can affect people's health. People younger than five and older than 65 are most likely to get sick from extreme heat. Low-income people are also at higher risk. They are less likely to be able to afford air-conditioning. So, they are less able to keep cool.

As average temperatures rise, the region's warm season is getting longer.

This change can cause problems. For example, it lengthens the allergy season. It also means insects such as mosquitoes can survive longer. In Montana, there could be four more weeks of mosquitoes each year. Mosquitoes can spread diseases to people. More days with mosquitoes means more chances of disease spreading.

When weather becomes hot, water **evaporates** more quickly. This can lead to droughts. Droughts are long periods of time that are much drier than usual. Crops need regular rainfall to grow well. A drought can make it hard for farmers to grow crops.

More than 82 percent of people in Wyoming live in an area at high risk for wildfires.

Drought can also increase the risk of wildfires. Dry forests burn more quickly. This leaves less time for people and animals to safely get away from a fire. Smoke from fire causes air pollution, too.

In addition, precipitation patterns are changing. Some parts of the region receive more snow in the winter and spring. These areas have less rain in the summer and fall. But the storms are often bigger. Heavy downpours are happening more often. They can cause **flash floods**.

## CAUSES OF CLIMATE CHANGE

Humans are causing climate change. People use huge amounts of fossil fuels. Cars, trucks, and planes burn fuel. Many power plants burn coal or natural gas. Burning fossil fuels puts greenhouse gases into the air. One main greenhouse gas is carbon dioxide. Greenhouse gases trap heat from the sun. That makes Earth hotter. It changes the climate in other ways, too. For example, glaciers are melting. That extra water is raising sea levels.

# THAT'S AMAZING!

# DALLAS GOLDTOOTH

Dallas Goldtooth is a member of the Mdewakanton (Mid-ah-*wah*-kah-ton) Dakota Nation. He is also part of the Diné Nation. Goldtooth teaches people how to speak the Dakota language.

Goldtooth is a climate **activist**, too. He brings Indigenous people together. They work to protect the environment. He often uses videos and social media. In this way, Goldtooth helps communities tell their stories.

Goldtooth worked to stop the Keystone XL pipeline. This pipeline was going to bring oil from Canada. It would have passed through tribal lands in Montana and South Dakota. When used, the oil would also have increased

Dallas Goldtooth is an activist, actor, poet, journalist, artist, and comedian.

greenhouse gas emissions. Also, pipelines often leak. Spilled oil can damage wetlands and other important habitats. Goldtooth helped in the fight against climate change. He also helped protect Indigenous lands.

CHAPTER 4

# SLOWING AND ADAPTING

To stop climate change, people must greatly reduce fossil fuel use. They can do this in many ways. For example, governments can shift to **renewable energy**. These kinds of energy do not release greenhouse gases.

Montana and South Dakota have long used hydropower. Hydropower makes

**The Confederated Salish and Kootenai Tribes run a hydro dam in Montana. It is the first major hydro dam to be tribally owned.**

23

electricity from water. Rivers flow through human-made dams. These dams have turbines. The water causes the turbines to turn. That rotation produces electricity.

Wind is another renewable source of energy. Wind power also involves spinning turbines. But it uses wind instead of water. States on the plains are very windy. As a result, wind power can produce lots of electricity. During the 2010s, plains states built many more wind turbines.

The northern Rockies and plains have other ways to reduce greenhouse gases. For example, agriculture is very important in the region. Farmers raise cattle, sheep,

In 2022, wind power supplied approximately one-third of North Dakota's electricity.

and pigs. Major crops include corn, wheat, and soybeans. Farming often produces methane and nitrous oxide. These are greenhouse gases.

Certain practices can lower emissions. For example, farmers can use fewer pesticides. These chemicals help protect crops from pests. But they also release nitrous oxide.

Some farming methods can both slow climate change and help people adapt to it. Crop rotation is one example. Crop rotation means changing the type of crop in a field from year to year. Certain crops use up some nutrients in the soil. Other crops put those nutrients back. When a field's crops rotate, the soil stays healthy. As a result, it holds more carbon. That helps slow climate change. Healthy soil also better survives extreme weather events such as droughts.

People can also help protect nature. For instance, wetlands are home to many kinds of birds. They also help store water. Protecting wetlands can make sure the

Many farms in Nebraska rotate corn and soybeans. Scientists suggest adding more crops to the rotation.

region has enough water. People can protect grasslands as well. Pronghorn and birds live in these areas.

Many Indigenous communities are working on adapting to climate change. The Apsáalooke (Up-*saw*-low-gah) live in Montana. The nation has experienced

In 2017, a severe drought hurt agriculture across North Dakota, South Dakota, and eastern Montana.

water quality problems for years. Climate change might make this problem worse. Spring flooding can pollute drinking water. Droughts can limit access to water. For these reasons, the Apsáalooke are working on restoring traditional sources of water.

The climate crisis is causing many changes across the northern Rockies and plains. But scientists and communities are hard at work in the region. They are focused on slowing climate change. They are also developing solutions to the changes that are already coming.

## HOW TO HELP

People of all ages can help deal with climate change. For example, young people can talk to their parents about the crisis. Research shows adults often listen most to their children about the issue. Young people can also write to local leaders. They can ask those leaders to act on climate change. Finally, young people can join protests. These actions help show the world that climate action matters.

# FOCUS ON
# THE NORTHERN ROCKIES AND PLAINS

*Write your answers on a separate piece of paper.*

1. Write a sentence describing the typical climate of the northern Rockies and plains.

2. What do you think is the best way to deal with climate change in the region? Why?

3. What is one of Montana's major sources of renewable energy?
   - A. hydropower
   - B. coal
   - C. natural gas

4. What makes the region a good place for wind power?
   - A. The region is near the ocean.
   - B. The Rockies have materials to build turbines.
   - C. The plains are very windy.

*Answer key on page 32.*

# GLOSSARY

**activist**
A person who takes action to make social or political changes.

**climate change**
A human-caused global crisis involving long-term changes in Earth's temperature and weather patterns.

**evaporates**
Changes from liquid to gas.

**flash floods**
Sudden rushes of water caused by heavy rain.

**humidity**
The amount of moisture in the air.

**Indigenous**
Native to a region, or belonging to ancestors who lived in a region before colonists arrived.

**precipitation**
Water that falls from clouds to the ground. It can be in the form of rain, hail, or snow.

**renewable energy**
Energy produced from a source that will not run out.

**reservoirs**
Human-made lakes used for water supply storage.

# TO LEARN MORE

## BOOKS

Cooke, Joanna. *Using Wind Turbines to Fight Climate Change*. Lake Elmo, MN: Focus Readers, 2023.

Minoglio, Andrea. *Our World Out of Balance: Understanding Climate Change and What We Can Do*. San Francisco: Blue Dot Kids Press, 2021.

Ternus, Lynn. *Nebraska*. Minneapolis: Abdo Publishing, 2023.

## NOTE TO EDUCATORS

Visit **www.focusreaders.com** to find lesson plans, activities, links, and other resources related to this title.

# INDEX

Apsáalooke, 27–28

Diné, 20
droughts, 17–18, 26, 28

floods, 5–7, 13, 19, 28

Goldtooth, Dallas, 20–21
Great Plains, 10–11

Keystone XL pipeline, 20

Mdewakanton Dakota, 20
Montana, 5, 10–12, 17, 20, 23, 27

Nebraska, 10–12
North Dakota, 9, 11

Rocky Mountains, 9–11, 13, 15, 24, 29

South Dakota, 10–11, 20, 23

wildfires, 18
Wyoming, 10–11

Yellowstone National Park, 6, 11

Answer Key: **1.** Answers will vary; **2.** Answers will vary; **3.** A; **4.** C